BAIL
a practical guide

BRIAN RAYMOND
Solicitor

Oyez Publishing Limited

© 1979

Oyez Publishing Limited,
Norwich House, 11/13 Norwich Street,
London EC4A 1AB

ISBN 0 85120 3981

Typeset by Millford Reprographics International Limited
Printed in Great Britain by T. J. Press (Padstow) Ltd,
Padstow, Cornwall.

BAIL
a practical guide

Contents

APPENDICES

1 Introduction

The question of bail, involving as it does, the liberty of the individual is one of central practical importance in a practitioner's criminal work and may occur unexpectedly in the civil field. Decisions have to be made quickly and without equivocation: a mistake at the outset of the proceedings can result in long periods in custody. This book is designed to provide the practitioner with all the technical information she or he is likely to need in making an effective application at the crucial moment, concentrating on practical steps to be taken, particularly in relation to an application before a Judge of the High Court in Chambers which can present problems even to the experienced. Naturally, this book will be concerned to a large degree with the detailed provisions of the Bail Act 1976, but, consideration will also be given to those instances where the old law still applies.

2 The Bail System –
When bail may be granted

A – By the Police

When there has been an arrest without a warrant the police have a substantial discretion as to whether to grant bail or not and this is governed by the Magistrates' Courts Act 1952, s38. They are not bound by the right to bail (see p14, below) and can either:

(*a*) keep the arrested person in custody and bring him before a magistrates' court 'as soon as practicable' (s38(4)); or (*b*) grant bail pending re-appearance at the police station if enquiries cannot be completed (s38 (2)); or

(*c*) grant bail pending an appearance at Court (s38 (1)).

Note that the police may require sureties to be taken but cannot impose conditions, such as a surrender of passport. Non-attendance involves possible prosecution for absconding (see p20, below) and the sureties are enforceable exactly as with bail granted by a court. Unlike a court, the police do not have to make a record of a refusal to grant bail but only of a decision to grant it.

B – Magistrates' Courts

Magistrates' courts have the power to remand in a wide variety of circumstances and by the Magistrates' Courts Act 1952, s105, the remand must either be on bail or in custody. It is important to distinguish between a remand and an adjournment: cases are *adjourned* when their hearings are temporarily halted and a future time fixed for their re-commencement, but defendants are *remanded* when the court imposes a personal requirement upon them to return on a future date and makes arrangements for their situation in the interim, ie by placing them on bail or in custody. When dealing with offences summarily the court is bound to remand the accused if the offence is one which is triable either way and the defendant has previously been remanded in custody or on bail by either the police or the court. Similarly the court must remand defendants when conducting proceedings preliminary to trial on indictment. The one exception is the case of a juvenile whose offence is being dealt with in summary fashion (Magistrates' Courts Act 1952, s14(4), as amended by the Criminal Law Act 1977). Thus if the defendant is charged with a purely summary offence, for example, the court need not remand him at all but have the option simply to adjourn the hearing until a further date and in appropriate cases advocates should urge that this be done.

Magistrates can also remand on bail after a custodial sentence has been imposed, pending appeal to the Crown Court or to the High Court by case stated (Magistrates' Courts Act 1952, s89). There is no power, however, for magistrates to grant bail pending an application for Judicial Review. The application must be made direct to the High Court (Criminal Justice Act 1948, s37).

C – 'Continuous Bail' and 'Paper Remands'

Any practitioner in magistrates' courts will be aware of how frequently appearances are *non-effective* and simply adjourned to a later date without anything significant taking place. These can often be anticipated and the courts have a useful power of remanding a defendant and extending his bail in his absence (Magistrates' Courts Act 1952, s106, as amended by Bail Act 1976, Sch 2, para 28), although in practice this power is used sparingly. If the defendant does not appear through illness or accident, the court can remand him in his absence, enlarging his sureties; in any other case it may appoint a later time for surrender, similarly enlarging the sureties. A diligent court will refuse to enlarge sureties unless satisfied that they are willing to have their responsibilities extended in this way and it is always prudent to obtain written consents from sureties before asking the court to adopt this course.

Even on occasions when the defendant's attendance is required, it may be possible and indeed desirable to dispense with the attendance of the sureties once bail has been granted. If bail is granted to a specific date (as it normally is) the responsibility of the surety extends only to that date and ends with the appearance of the defendant. If bail is to be re-granted, the surety must sign his recognizance once again. To avoid the complications of arranging for this to happen on each remand, a surety can be made *continuous* in order that the person so bailed appears:

> at every time and place to which during the course of the proceedings the hearing may from time to time be adjourned and also before the Crown Court in the event of the person so bailed being committed for trial there. (Magistrates' Courts Act 1952, s105(3)(*c*)).

Thus the sureties need not attend again even at committal, although once again they should be clear about what they are letting themselves in for. The term *continuous bail* is slightly misleading as it only really refers to the position of the sureties if bail is re-granted to the defendant on future remands: the court is perfectly free to remand in custody on a future occasion, notwithstanding that bail has been made continuous on an earlier hearing. The period of continuity ceases, however, on the first appearance at the Crown Court and sureties will have to attend if bail is to be renewed during the trial or to a further appearance.

D – The Crown Court

The Crown Court can, subject to certain limitations, grant bail before, during and after the hearing of any matter committed to it (Courts Act 1971, s13(4)). Bail can be granted on committals for trial, sentence or Borstal recommendation etc where the defendant has been remanded in custody by the committing court or when an appeal is pending after a custodial sentence has been imposed. Thus the defendant in the magistrates' court who receives a prison sentence can apply for bail pending appeal to the magistrates' court or to the Crown Court or to both. After the Crown Court has dealt with the matter, whether it is a trial or a matter of sentencing, such as a breach of Probation Order or breach of Community Service Order, its powers to grant bail are more limited and can only be used when the defendant has applied for a case to be stated to the High Court or has applied for certiorari etc. Bail pending appeal to the Court of Appeal is dealt with by that court.

It should be noted that the Bail Act 1976 applies up to the moment of conviction and thus serves to overrule the guidance in the Home Office circular No 104/1972 in which it is stated that bail during the trial itself is in the discretion of the trial judge and that it should not be granted during lunch if there is a possibility of contact with witnesses and jurors. In fact, the judge must exercise his discretion in accordance with the Bail Act, and can only refuse bail for the prescribed reasons.

E – The High Court

The High Court has a general supervisory jurisdiction over the granting of bail by magistrates' courts by virtue of the Criminal Justice Act 1967, s22:

> Where in connection with any criminal proceedings a magistrates' court has power to admit any person to bail, but either refuses to do so or does so on terms unacceptable to him, the High Court may grant him bail or when he has been granted bail, may vary any conditions on which bail was granted.

Thus the High Court, which exercises its power through a single judge sitting in chambers, can review the operation of the magistrates' court in respect of the granting of bail at any stage, including committal to the Crown Court for trial or sentence and bail pending appeal to the Crown Court or to the High Court itself by certiorari or case stated. Note that the procedure cannot be used to challenge the decision of the Crown Court and once bail has been refused by a judge in chambers a defendant shall not be entitled to a fresh application to any other judge or to the Divisional Court. Thus if a defendant, committed for trial in custody, applies immediately to a judge in chambers and is unsuccessful, he cannot then exercise his right to apply to the Crown Court for bail (RSC Ord 79, r9(12)). On the other hand, r9(12) does not prevent further applications to the same judge sitting in chambers, although this may not be easy in the provinces where High Court judges will only be sitting for a limited period at any one time. The decision to apply to a judge in chambers should not be taken lightly as the consequences of an adverse decision may be severe in that courts may feel that the decision of a judge in chambers is final and binding upon them. A further drawback which will be only too familiar to practitioners is that legal aid is unavailable and the application must either be provided as a free service or funded privately by the defendant.

F – The Court of Appeal

As the power of the Crown Court to grant bail post-conviction is limited to where there is a pending application for certiorari or appeal by way of case stated, the power to grant bail pending an application to the Court of Appeal lies with that court itself. By the Criminal Appeal Act 1968, s19:

> The Court of Appeal, may, if they think fit, on the application of the appellant, grant him bail pending the determination of the appeal.

This power is exercisable either by the full court or by a single judge sitting alone. It is by now well established that the Court of Appeal is most reluctant to grant bail save in exceptional circumstances and no application has any prospect of success save against the background of very powerful and persuasive grounds of appeal. The court has recently re-affirmed this test and stated that it has not been altered by recent legislation. Thus the granting of leave to appeal against sentence does not, of itself constitute 'exceptional circumstances' (*R* v *Walton*, CA 18 December 1978).

3 Procedure

A – Magistrates' Courts

There is no set procedure for the making of a bail application before magistrates. No notice of intention to apply for bail need be given as the court is now compelled to consider the question of bail on each appearance, whether there is an application or not (Bail Act 1976, s4). The normal pattern will be for the bench to ask the prosecutor if there are any objections to bail, and then to ask the defendant or his representative if an application is to be made. At this point certain regional differences of practice become relevant: in London and other major cities, the officer in the case will enter the witness box (although not necessarily take the oath) and having given objections will allow himself to be questioned by the defence. Some courts, however, have evolved the practice whereby the objections are given from the well of the court and no questioning is allowed. As there are no rules or even guidelines on this point, the bench have a total discretion as to the procedure to be followed, although it is suggested that a method whereby the prosecution's contentions can be tested by examination must be preferable to one which does not allow this facility.

The only situation where prior notice need be given is when the defence or prosecution intend to apply for the grant or variation of bail (under the Bail Act 1976, s3(8)) on an occasion other than a designated appearance. This might occur, for example, when a defendant has been granted bail for an extended period and wishes to make an alteration in his conditions of bail, or when a newly arrested defendant is remanded in custody for eight days when unrepresented and, on receiving advice, wishes to make an application before he is next due to appear in court. In these circumstances, adequate notice must be given to the other side (at least twenty-four hours) and similarly to the court, so that the relevant charge sheet and section of the register can be made ready. There are no prescribed forms and ordinary letters will suffice. The application will then be heard before the court's normal business for the day.

It often happens that a relatively trifling alteration in a defendant's terms of bail is required, a change of address or time of reporting for example, which is unopposed by the prosecution and yet requires the formal sanction of the court before it can take effect. Personal application in these circumstances can often be avoided if the solicitor for the defendant, having first obtained the consent of the prosecution, simply writes to the Clerk to the Justices of the court concerned (or the Chief Clerk in Inner London) and asks if the necessary change can be made without the necessity of either party attending. Most courts will readily agree to this and the method can be employed in the Crown Court as well with even greater savings of time and trouble.

B – The Crown Court

Appearances at the Crown Court will of necessity be far less frequent than at the magistrates' court and thus the court will usually only consider the question of bail when specifically requested to do so by the defence. Having decided to make the application, the defendant must first ascertain that the court will be able to entertain the application on the desired day as there may be no judge available or too many applications listed already. If the court agrees to the application being made, full details should be given on the telephone to enable the court to make provisional arrangements. Immediately following this, Notice of Application should be despatched to the court, the prosecution and the Director of Public Prosecutions if they are acting, so that they are received not less than twenty-four hours before the application is to be made. The form of notice is set out in Appendix B to this work (see p60). It will be seen that the information required is fairly straightforward except for the last requirement – 'state fully, facts relied upon and list previous convictions (if any). Give details of proposed sureties and answer any objections raised previously'. Clearly it is not necessary to rehearse every argument to be used, the main point of the question being to provide notice to the prosecution of the factual content so that this may be verified if necessary before the hearing. It would be pedantic in the extreme if any court were to decline to listen to an argument because it was not listed on the form and the applicant may confine himself to listing sureties (with full names, addresses and dates of birth), previous convictions and available employment and accommodation etc.

The prosecution, on receipt of the notice can either:

 (*a*) indicate to the court and the applicant that he will be represented at the hearing; or

 (*b*) indicate that there are no objections to the application; or

 (*c*) provide a written statement of reasons for opposing the application to both court and defendant.

In practice, the prosecution will always appear if there are any contested issues and it should be assumed that they will do so unless notified to the contrary. The appellant himself, however, if in custody will not be brought up to the court for the application unless the Crown Court itself gives leave. This will only be given for a reason more substantial than the fact that he would like a day out of prison, or that there is a possibility of a need to take instructions at the hearing.

C – Judge in Chambers

The basic outlines of the procedure are set out in RSC Ord 79 r9. In order to commence the procedure, you will need:

 (*a*) Summons in form 97 (where bail has been refused altogether) or form 97A in the *Supreme Court Practice* (where a variation of terms is sought); see Appendix B, below;

 (*b*) Affidavit in support.

Forms 97 and 97A, as they appear in Appendix B have been amended to comply with the terms of the Bail Act. The summons should be served upon the prosecution twenty-four hours before the application is to be made. It must first be issued at the Crown Office which will insert the venue and the name of the judge before whom it is to be heard. If the Crown Office is approached less than twenty-four hours before the application is to be made, it will require an assurance that the prosecution have agreed to accept shorter notice. *The affidavit* (a suggested form is set out in *Chitty and Jacob* at 1366 and 1368) need not be served with the summons, but should be made available to the prosecution before going in front of the judge. The affidavit can either be of the defendant himself, although the logistics of this will be difficult to arrange in most cases, or by the solicitors representing him. It should set out in full the history of the matter insofar as it relates to the granting of bail and detail any previous applications together with the objections raised. Full details of sureties, accommodation available and suggested conditions must be set out in the affidavit. The affidavit should contain information rather than argument as the argument can be presented orally before the judge himself. The application may be made by either a barrister or a solicitor or by the applicant himself where a variation is sought. No other persons are allowed to attend the hearing. The judge is to be addressed as 'My Lord'.

The prudent practitioner will arm himself with two copies of a draft order as this will be required if bail is granted. The form of the order is No 98 or 98A in the *Supreme Court Practice* and these are set out in Appendix B, below. Once bail has been granted, or a variation obtained, the precise form of the order should be completed (in manuscript if necessary) and submitted to the associates sitting with the judge for approval. When this has been obtained two copies of the order must be submitted to the Crown Office where one will be stamped and returned to the applicant. There is no fee payable on the issue of the order although the summons presented at the outset of the proceedings will have to be stamped £1.

In relation to bail granted by a judge in chambers the recognizances of the sureties should not be taken unless twenty-four hours' notice of intention to do so has been served upon the prosecution (RSC Ord 79 r9(7) as substituted by SI 1978 No 251). This also applies to bail granted by the Crown Court (Crown Court Rules 1971, r17, as substituted by SI 1978 No 439). In each case the authority granting bail has the power to direct that this requirement shall not apply and in practice, the observance of this requirement is not always demanded.

D – The Court of Appeal

1 Under Legal Aid

Where the applicant is dependent on legal aid, intention to apply for bail must be noted upon the form N and this must be accompanied by Notice of Intention to Apply for Bail in form B as reproduced in Appendix B, below. Bail will not be considered without the submission of forms N and G and grounds settled by counsel. The consideration of bail will be by a single judge sitting in private at the normal time. The Registrar's staff naturally give priority to cases where the sentence is short but nevertheless, there is likely to be a substantial delay following the submission of the application and its consideration by the single judge.

2 *Where the Solicitor is Privately Instructed*

Where the defendant can instruct a solicitor privately or where the solicitor is prepared to make the application without payment, a more rapid method may be used. This too must begin with the submission of forms N and G together with the appropriate grounds as settled by counsel and then by form B (Appendix B, below) which must also be served upon the prosecution not less than twenty-four hours before the application is to be made. A time for the hearing of the application (probably early in the morning before a judge commences his normal business for the day) will then be agreed between the defence and prosecution usually with the assistance of counsel's clerk. The Criminal Appeal Rules 1968 (SI 1968 No 1262) prescribe a twenty-four hour period of notice which is likely to be necessary so that the papers relating to the case can be obtained from the Crown Court. In an urgent case, however, where there are overwhelming grounds of appeal and it is clear that a strong application for bail may be made, the procedure may be shortened with the consent of the prosecution, by appearing before a judge in summary fashion, outside normal court hours if necessary. There is always a judge on duty for this purpose and he may be contacted through the Royal Courts of Justice.

E – After the Successful Application – How to obtain release

In bail matters the practitioner will frequently find that he is involved in far more work after a successful application than before because of the difficulties in actually securing his client's release. The problem revolves around the taking of sureties or the fulfilling of conditions precedent, such as the surrender of a passport. If the sureties are present in court the matter will be resolved swiftly and the defendant released immediately if he is present. The difficulties arise if bail is granted subject to sureties to be taken later or at another place.

1 *The Taking of Sureties (Bail Act 1976, s8)*

Where a court grants bail on the condition that sureties for attendance are forthcoming, the sureties may be taken by either:

(*a*) a Justice of the Peace;

(*b*) a Justice's Clerk;

(*c*) a Police Inspector or a Police Officer in charge of a police station;

(*d*) the Governor of a prison or Remand Centre;

(*e*) an officer of the Crown Court (for proceedings in the Crown Court);

(*f*) the Registrar of Criminal Appeals (for bail pending appeal to the Court of Appeal).

If any of the prescribed persons will not accept the proposed surety, the surety can apply to either:

(*a*) the original court which granted bail; or

(*b*) the magistrates' court for the Petty Session Area in which he (the surety) resides.

2 Obtaining Release

After the sureties have signed on and been accepted, what then? Release of the applicant, who will by this time have oeen taken back to his remand prison, is not automatic. The governor of the prison does not have to allow release until he is 'satisfied that the recognizances of all sureties required have been taken and that all requirements have been complied with' (Magistrates' Courts Rules 1968, r74, as substituted by SI 1978 No 147). This may be less than easy to achieve if a court in London has granted bail subject to sureties taken in Leeds and Bristol, for example.

The system prescribed by the Magistrates' Court and Crown Court Rules is extremely pedestrian and could result in delay of several days before the applicant is released. At each level when bail is granted by a court, a prescribed form of order is to be sent by the court to the prison and a certificate is issued as to the sureties required. No person who is asked to take a surety need do so without the certificate. After the surety has been taken, a copy of the recognizance is sent to the court and another copy to the prison, upon receipt of which the defendant should be released.

It will be appreciated that this procedure, if followed to the letter, would take several days to complete, during which time the defendant would languish in prison. An attempt to alleviate this problem was made by the Home Office in their circular No 104 of 1972 which suggests that the passage of the various notices and recognizances could be anticipated with the use of telephone calls by which the governor would be informed:

(*a*) that the court had granted bail on particular terms; and

(*b*) at the appropriate time, that sureties had signed their recognizances.

Experience has shown, however, that this relies heavily upon the co-operation of the police and the willingness of the prison governor to accept the information in this way. It is therefore preferable to arrange for an energetic and mobile friend of the defendant to collect and deliver the documentation. Rather than have to repeat this process on each remand, a wise practitioner will ensure that bail is *continuous* so that renewal is automatic.

F – Legal Aid

1 Magistrates' Courts

If legal aid is granted for the proceedings themselves it will cover any application for bail and under the Bail Act 1976, s11 makes the grant of legal aid compulsory in certain circumstances:

(*a*) when a person charged with an offence before a magistrates' court is brought before the court in pursuance of a remand in custody on an occasion when he may again be remanded or committed in custody, if he was not represented on the previous remand; and

(*b*) on a post-conviction remand for reports in either the Crown Court or magistrates' court where it is proposed that the remand be in custody.

Note that in relation to (*a*) the compulsory legal aid extends only 'for the purpose of so much of the proceedings as are related to bail' and courts are specifically reminded that the compulsory legal aid for bail applications does not require them to grant legal aid for the proceedings themselves.

The Act does not make it clear whether such *bail only* legal aid certificates apply only to the hearing upon which their grant is compulsory or all subsequent hearings as well. It is suggested that the reference to 'proceedings' refers to every appearance until the matter is finalised and thus a *bail only* certificate will cover bail applications wherever they are relevant. Curiously this provision does not extend to the Crown Court, presumably because the number of unrepresented defendants is very small.

2 Crown Court

Legal aid for the proceedings themselves will cover bail applications made to the court for both ordinary designated appearances and special bail applications (*Archbold*, para 310). Repeated bail applications may be difficult to justify on taxation, however, unless a change of circumstances can be shown. Experience shows, however, that where legal aid is granted for two counsel the taxing authorities will normally allow at least one application for bail by leading counsel without the need for special justification.

3 Judge in Chambers

The ordinary criminal legal aid for proceedings in the magistrates' court or Crown Court does not extend to the making of applications before a judge in chambers. As this is a High Court procedure, civil legal aid is in theory available but most area committees will decline to grant legal aid on the ground that an alternative method exists in the form of an application via the Official Solicitor (RSC Ord 79, r9(4)). By this, a defendant may apply to the Official Solicitor to make a bail application to the judge in chambers on his behalf and the application is usually made in written form based upon information supplied by the defendant. The chances of success by this method are very poor indeed, as one might expect from a procedure where there is no advocacy on behalf of the applicant. However, there is also a serious danger in the use of this method: ineffective or not, an application by means of the Official Solicitor is still an application to the judge in chambers and this serves to prevent any further application before another judge. Thus if bail is refused on committal, a defendant who is persuaded by misguided prison staff to request the assistance of the Official Solicitor in a futile application, may well forfeit his right to apply to a judge of the Crown Court for which his normal legal aid will enable him to be properly represented.

4 Court of Appeal

Under the normal procedure the application for leave to appeal will also comprise an application for legal aid and this will be dealt with by the single judge. The Registrar will not normally grant legal aid for the purpose of making a bail application before the matter has been considered in toto by the single judge.

4 The Right to Bail

By far the most important innovation of the Bail Act 1976 is the creation, in certain situations, of a *right* to bail which the court can only over-ride in clearly defined circumstances or for designated reasons. Note that the Act only applies to criminal proceedings – the automatic right to bail does not exist in any civil proceedings.

A – When Does it Apply?

(*a*) On any appearance before a magistrates' court or Crown Court in the course of, or in connection with, the proceedings for an offence (s4(2)(*a*)); or

(*b*) when a bail application is made in respect of the proceedings (s4(2)(*b*));

(*c*) to remands after convictions for reports to be made (s4(4));

(*d*) to appearances before a court for breach of Probation or Community Service Orders, including committals to the Crown Court for this purpose (s4(3)).

B – When Does it Not Apply? (s4)

(*a*) To proceedings after conviction (subject to the specific exceptions above);

(*b*) to extradition or fugitive offender's proceedings;

(*c*) to committals to the Crown Court for sentence or with recommendations for Borstal training or as an 'incorrigible rogue' or 'idle and disorderly' under the Vagrancy Acts;

(*d*) on appeal to the Crown Court or Divisional Court where a custodial sentence is imposed;

(*e*) on committal to the Crown Court for breach of a suspended sentence to be dealt with;

(*f*) to police bail in any form.

When the presumption exists, the court must make its decision in accordance with the strict terms of the Bail Act 1976 and must grant bail unless one of the exceptions is applicable (see p15, below). Thus objections must be made by the prosecution before the application is presented, as in the absence of any kind of representations to the contrary, the court will have no information upon which to invoke the exceptions. Where the presumption in favour of bail applies, it is for the court to justify a remand in custody rather than for the defence to apply for a remand on bail in the first instance. Note that the presumption applies in the Crown Court up to the moment of conviction: keeping the defendant in custody over lunch to avoid contact with jurors or during the judge's summing up to accord with normal practice and for no other reason is simply not in accordance with the Act.

C – Reasons for Refusal

Having established that the proceedings are criminal and the situation is one where the presumption in favour of bail applies, the court is then compelled to grant bail unless one of the exceptions to the grant of bail, contained in the Bail Act 1976, Sch 1, is established. There are two overlapping sets of exceptions to cover offences that are both 'imprisonable' and 'non-imprisonable'. To decide into which category the offence falls, no regard is to be paid to 'any enactment prohibiting or restricting imprisonment of young offenders or first offenders' and thus the issue is not whether the particular defendant can be sent to prison but whether a prison sentence can be imposed in any circumstances whatsoever.

There are three exceptions common to both categories, five which apply to imprisonable offences only and one which applies to non-imprisonable offences only.

1 Exceptions Common to Both Categories

(*a*) That the defendant has been arrested for breaking bail in relation to the same offence (Sch 1 Pt I para 6, Pt II para 5). The schedule refers to an arrest under s7 which empowers arrest not only for actual failure to attend or absenting oneself during the hearing, but also for an anticipated non-surrender, an actual or anticipated breach of the conditions of bail and the withdrawal of a surety. Note that the simple fact of an arrest under this section which may prove to be wholly unjustified, serves to remove the presumption in favour of bail for all future remands, and should be avoided;

(*b*) that a remand in custody is necessary for the defendant's own protection (adults) or welfare (juveniles);

(*c*) that the defendant is in custody in pursuance of the sentence of a court or any authority acting under any of the Services Acts. Note that this exception only refers to actual sentences: committals for non-payment of fines, or maintenance do not fall within the exception and neither do other remands in custody for other offences.

2 Exceptions for Imprisonable Offences Only

The first three of the five exceptions under this category of the Bail Act 1976, Sch 1, form the issues that invariably lie at the heart of the contested bail application. They relate to the defendant's future conduct and the test applied is whether the court is satisfied that there are substantial grounds for believing that they would occur if the defendant was released on bail (whether subject to conditions or not):

(*a*) that the defendant will fail to surrender to custody; or

(*b*) that the defendant will commit an offence while on bail; or

(*c*) that the defendant will interfere with witnesses or otherwise obstruct the course of justice.

The remaining two exceptions relate to the practicability of obtaining information about the defendant:

(*d*) that it has not been practicable to obtain sufficient information for the purpose of taking the bail decision due to lack of time since the start of the proceedings against him; or

(*e*) where the case is adjourned for enquiries or a report after conviction and it is impracticable to complete the enquiries or make the report unless the defendant is in custody.

3 *Exception for Non-imprisonable Offences Only*

This exception is a modified form of (*a*), above – 'will fail to surrender to custody' and is the only one of the central trio of exceptions applicable to imprisonable offences. It also applies, albeit in a qualified form, to the non-imprisonable category. The court is required first to establish a premise – that the defendant has previously broken bail and from that infer a conclusion that the defendant would fail to surrender to custody. The possibility of further offences or the interference with witnesses is thus not relevant to this category of offences.

5 Making the Application

A – The Shape of the Argument

From the above it will be seen that the main impact of the Bail Act 1976 is to impose a fairly rigid framework of ideas around the basic decision of whether to grant bail or not. Since the Act has been in force experience has shown that the majority of arguments revolve around the central three exceptions relating to future conduct and if any of the other exceptions are invoked, controversy is normally limited.

There is still, however, a tendency to confuse the three basic reasons for refusal of bail (which are all the statute allow) and the factors which are evidence in support of those reasons. No fixed abode, or the seriousness of the offence are not exceptions to the statutory right of bail. They are factors which could be considered to support, for example, the likelihood of absconding or further offences being committed. Bail applications should not be allowed to become disputes over these matters of evidence unless their relevance to the three primary exceptions can be established.

The Act allows the court a fairly free hand in relation to the factors it can consider in deciding whether the exceptions apply, permitting 'any considerations which appear to be relevant', but it also sets out a schedule of points for the purpose of guidance (Sch 1 Pt I para 9):

    (*a*) the nature and seriousness of the offence and the probable sentence;

    (*b*) the character, antecedents, associations, and community ties of the defendant;

    (*c*) any record of jumping bail in the past;

    (*d*) the strength of the evidence.

B – Conditions of Bail

Only a court has the power to impose conditions of bail whereas the police are limited to requiring sureties if necessary. Practitioners will be familiar with the type of conditions that courts like to impose such as reporting to the police, residing at a particular address or even a *curfew*. The Bail Act, s3(6) requires that conditions shall only be imposed if necessary to prevent the three occurrences which form the main exceptions to the right to bail, namely:

    (*a*) failure to surrender to custody;

    (*b*) the committing of further offences while on bail;

    (*c*) interference with witnesses or obstruction of the course of justice;

or in a case of a post-conviction remand for reports to ensure that:

    (*d*) the defendant makes himself available for the purpose of enabling enquiries or a report to be made to assist the court in dealing with him for the offence.

Experienced practitioners will know that benches often like to be presented with a *package* of proposed conditions and sureties, particularly in a difficult case. Although the Act in no way restricts the ingenuity of the advocate in devising conditions to satisfy the court, it may be used to restrain the imposition of a condition which appears to be merely punitive in its effect. If, after bail has been granted, a particular condition is found to be too onerous or simply unnecessary, the defendant can apply to the court at any time for variation (s3(8)) and the prosecution may similarly apply for extra conditions to be imposed. When conditions of bail are imposed by a magistrates' court the dissatisfied defendant can apply to a judge in chambers for a variation in exactly the same way as when there is a complete refusal of bail.

6 Recording of Decisions and the Giving of Reasons

A - Recording Decisions (s5(1))

The bail decision must be recorded in the prescribed manner in the register and the defendant must be provided with a copy of the record on request, when:

(*a*) a court or constable grants bail; or

(*b*) a court withholds bail from a person to whom the presumption in favour of bail applies; or

(*c*) a court officer or constable appoints a place for surrender to bail or changes a place or time already fixed; or

(*d*) a court imposes or varies conditions of bail.

Note that the police are only required to record the granting of bail and not its refusal.

B - The Giving of Reasons (s5(3))

The police are wholly exempt from this requirement which only applies to magistrates' and Crown Courts. Here reasons must be stated when:

(*a*) bail is withheld; or

(*b*) conditions are imposed in granting bail de novo; or

(*c*) when conditions are imposed or varied in pre-existing bail.

The function of s5(3) is to enable the defendant to 'consider making an application in the matter to another court'. Thus the information is primarily directed to the mind of the defendant and should be in terms comprehensible to him and at the same time be within the terms of the Act. Form 146 C in the *Magistrates' Courts Forms*, (record of decision to withhold bail) requires reference to specific paragraphs within Sch 1 and to the reasons for applying such exception. Courts are free to design their own forms, but they must be similar in effect to form 146 C. Reasons that are vague or outside Sch 1 should not be accepted.

C - Recording Reasons

Where a court is required to give reasons for its bail decisions, the prescribed record of the decision should include a note of the reasons given and this must be presented to the defendant whether he asks for it or not (s5(4)). The only exception to this is for represented defendants in the Crown Court where the note will only be provided on request (s5(5)). In practice this means that the court has to give every defendant who is refused bail or granted bail subject to conditions a suitably annotated copy of form 146 C. The system adopted by magistrates' courts since the Act has been in force involves the use of forms on self duplicating paper of different colours. The defendant's copy is pink in some parts of London although other permutations are used elsewhere. Note that there is no necessity to provide a copy of the form for a remand on unconditional bail. In many courts, particularly in London, the reasons are usually entered upon the register and one copy of the bail form is attached to the charge sheet by the clerk. Thus an inspection of the clerk's papers will reveal a continuing history of the bail conditions in a particular case.

7 Enforcing Attendance

A – The New Offence of Absconding

Major changes have been made by the Bail Act 1976, to the system of ensuring that the bailed defendant observes the terms of his conditions of bail. The main duty of the bailed defendant is to surrender to the custody of the court or police at the prescribed time and place (s3). The practice of taking a recognizance from the defendant has now been abolished for bail in criminal proceedings and has been replaced by the duty, when granted bail, to surrender to custody at the appointed place and time. This is enforced by the corresponding offence of failing to surrender to custody, or *absconding* under s6. This is an entirely new creation of the Act and is punishable as a wholly separate matter from the offence in respect of which bail was originally granted.

The offence is committed when the defendant on bail either:

(*a*) fails without reasonable cause to surrender to custody (s6(1)); or (*b*) having failed to surrender to custody with reasonable cause, then further fails to surrender as soon after the appointed time as is reasonably practicable (s6(2)).

These are alternative offences, but the prima facie evidence (ie failure to surrender) will be the same for both of them.

Courts may proceed with both offences as a matter of routine and continue only with s6(1),(2) if reasonable cause is established. The offence is committed as soon as there has been a failure to surrender but it is clear that an early attempt to get to court will offer substantial mitigation of the offence although the Act makes no specific provision for this.

'The reasonable cause' justifying an initial failure to surrender need not be identical with the considerations affecting the practicability of a rapid surrender thereafter. The onus of proof of reasonable cause rests upon the defendant (s6(3)) so that the prosecution will be able to establish a prima facie case purely on proof of failure to appear. On the other hand once reasonable cause is established, the onus is on the prosecution to prove that surrender was not as soon as practicable thereafter. Note that the offence relates to police bail as well as to appearances at court.

The offence may be dealt with summarily, when it is punishable by up to three months' imprisonment, or a £400 fine or both. However it may be dealt with as a criminal contempt of court in which case the maxima are 12 months and an unlimited fine or both (s6(7)). When the defendant is convicted of the offence by a magistrates' court, that court may commit for sentence in the normal way when powers of punishment are felt to be inadequate or when the defendant is committed for trial on the main offence (s6(6)(*a*) and (*b*)).

B – Actual or Anticipated Breaches of Bail

1 Non-Attendance

The offence created by the Bail Act 1976, s6 does not of itself carry a power of arrest without warrant. It is only when the defendant fails to turn up at the appointed place and time that the court may issue a warrant, commonly referred to as *a bench warrant* for the defendant's arrest (s7(1)). This is also possible if the defendant having arrived at court, absents himself from it before his case is heard. In either case the warrant may be *backed for bail*, ie contain an endorsement to the effect that the defendant who is apprehended is to be released (with or without sureties) pending his re-appearance at court. In the absence of circumstances tending to show reasons for the non-appearance, the court is not likely to order the warrant to be endorsed in this way. These warrants are, of course, for failure to appear as required by the Act and are a completely separate matter from a warrant issued for the offence itself.

2 Arrest for Breach of Bail

The Bail Act 1976, s7 re-enacts the pre-existing powers of arrest without warrant, by a police constable who has reasonable grounds for belief that either:

(*a*) the bailed person is not likely to surrender to custody; or

(*b*) the bailed person is likely to or has already broken a condition of his bail; or

(*c*) a surety has notified him that he wishes to withdraw on the grounds of the surety's belief that the defendant will not attend.

After an arrest under this section, the defendant must be brought before the magistrates' court for the area of the arrest within twenty-four hours, unless he was arrested within twenty-four hours of the time of his normal appearance at court when he should be taken to the court to which he was originally bailed. Note that even where a defendant is bailed to a Crown Court he can be brought before the local magistrates' court when apprehended in this way (s7(4)).

When such a defendant is brought before the court, it must decide how to remand him henceforth. The Act requires the court to consider the question of future bail in a special way; it must first decide if he is either:

(*a*) not likely to surrender to custody; or

(*b*) in breach or likely to be in breach of terms of bail.

If the answer is 'No' to all these questions the court is required to re-grant bail on the same terms hitherto. If either of these questions can be answered in the affirmative, the court has a totally free hand and can grant bail or withhold it as it thinks fit. The presumption in favour of bail does not of course apply here as this situation (ie after an arrest under s7) is one of the exceptions to the general right to bail for both imprisonable and non-imprisonable offences. However the court should be persuaded to enquire into the circumstances of the arrest where the breach was either technical or otherwise venial.

C – Sureties

The Bail Act, 1976 requires the conditions of bail to be imposed only in clearly defined circumstances, but the question of whether to require sureties in order to re-enforce the defendant's personal duty to surrender is left entirely within the discretion of the court or police and the Act provides no guidance at all (s3(4)).
Criteria are laid down, however, for the assessment of the suitability of proposed sureties (s8(2)):

    (*a*) the sureties' financial resources;

    (*b*) his character and any previous convictions; and

    (*c*) his proximity (whether in point of kinship, place of residence or otherwise) to the person for whom he is to be surety. These considerations are by no means exclusive but serve to dispel the old myth still found among members of the police force that sureties have to be male house-holders of unblemished character. The Act also sanctions the practice of granting bail subject to sureties to be taken later (s3(4)). The procedure in relation to this is discussed at p10, above. There is also provision for sureties to be taken in Scotland in respect of proceedings taking place in England and Wales (s8(6)).
In general a surety is only responsible for the defendant's actual appearance in court at the specified time or times, regardless of whether the ancillary conditions of bail are adhered to. However, the Bail Act 1976, s3(7) provides in the case of a juvenile, for the parents of the defendant to secure by their own recognizance the compliance of their off-spring with any condition of bail imposed by the Court. The parents must agree to being so bound and the requirement cannot cover any matter 'to which the parents' consent does not extend'. The amount of recognizance may not exceed £50.

D – Indemnifying Sureties

The indemnification of bail has always been an offence at common law and the Act creates a statutory offence of 'agreeing to indemnify sureties' (s9). The essence of the offence is the agreement (whether actual performance takes place or not) between persons to indemnify an existing or potential surety against any liability which the surety may incur. The agreement may take place before or after the person becomes a surety and the offence is committed if it contemplates compensation in money or money's worth. Both the surety and the person offering indemnity are guilty of the offence. It is interesting that the offence consists solely of the prior agreement and that the obligation is referred to in the future tense; this indicates that an actual payment without earlier agreement where liability has already been incurred will not be caught by this section. The offence is punishable summarily by 3 months' imprisonment or a fine of up to £400 or both and by 12 months' imprisonment or an unlimited fine or both in the Crown Court. The consent of the Director of Public Prosecutions is necessary before proceedings may be commenced.

E – Security Given by or on Behalf of the Defendant

One of the most significant features introduced by the Bail Act 1976 is that the defendant can now be required to give some security as a pre-condition of bail. This had hitherto been impossible, but the Act allows the court to request that the security be given where 'it appears that he is unlikely to remain in Great Britain until the time appointed for him to surrender to custody' (s3(5)). In this context 'Great Britain' includes only England, Scotland and Wales.

This provision offers great scope for defendants of foreign nationality who, although persons of substance, are without a fixed address or close friends in this country who will be able to act as surety. By depositing a substantial sum they will be able to satisfy the court of their intention to return. Section 3(5) will also apply to a person of British nationality who is ordinarily resident overseas such as a tax exile or a person who works abroad. The deposit of security will obviously be a condition precedent to the grant of bail and will have to be completed before the defendant can be released from custody.

It is important to note that in contra-distinction to the strictly personal liability of the surety, the security offered 'may be given by him or on his behalf' and thus may be money or property brought specifically into the country for this purpose. Money will clearly be the most acceptable form of security but there is no reason why the court should not accept house deeds, share certificates etc. There may be difficulty over valuable items of a non-documentary nature such as jewellery, but there is no statutory bar to their acceptance.

The quantum to be deposited is clearly within the court's discretion, but it can be argued that the deposit of security should approximate to the size of the surety which would otherwise be required, particularly if property is deposited by a person other than the defendant. Advocates should always encourage the courts to grant bail by making an offer of a deposit of security where it is feasible and relevant.

Appendix A
Bail Act 1976

The text of the Bail Act 1976 has been amended to take account of the amending provisions of the Criminal Law Act 1977, Sch 12. These amendments appear in square brackets.

This Act has been reproduced by courtesy of HMSO.

PRELIMINARY

1. Meaning of "bail in criminal proceedings"

(1) In this Act "bail in criminal proceedings" means—

(*a*) bail grantable in or in connection with proceedings for an offence to a person who is accused or convicted of the offence, or

(*b*) bail grantable in connection with an offence to a person who is under arrest for the offence or for whose arrest for the offence a warrant (endorsed for bail) is being issued.

(2) In this Act "bail" means bail grantable under the law (including common law) for the time being in force.

(3) Except as provided by section 13(3) of this Act, this section does not apply to bail in or in connection with proceedings outside England and Wales.

(4) This section does not apply to bail granted before the coming into force of this Act.

(5) This section applies—

(*a*) whether the offence was committed in England or Wales or elsewhere, and

(*b*) whether it is an offence under the law of England and Wales, or of any other country or territory.

(6) Bail in criminal proceedings shall be granted (and in particular shall be granted unconditionally or conditionally) in accordance with this Act.

2. Other definitions

(1) In this Act, unless the context otherwise requires, "conviction" includes—

    (*a*) a finding of guilt,

    (*b*) a finding that a person is not guilty by reason of insanity,

    (*c*) a finding under section 26(1) of the Magistrates' Courts Act 1952 (remand for medical examination) that the person in question did the act or made the omission charged, and

    (*d*) a conviction of an offence for which an order is made placing the offender on probation or discharging him absolutely or conditionally,

and "convicted" shall be construed accordingly.

(2) In this Act, unless the context otherwise requires—

"child" means a person under the age of fourteen,

"court" includes a judge of a court [or] a justice of the peace and, in the case of a specified court, includes a judge or (as the case may be) justice having powers to act in connection with proceedings before that court.

"Courts-Martial Appeal rules" means rules made under section 49 of the Courts-Martial (Appeals) Act 1968,

"Crown Court rules" means rules made under section 15 of the Courts Act 1971,

"magistrates' courts rules" means rules made under section 15 of the Justices of the Peace Act 1949,

"offence" includes an alleged offence,

"proceedings against a fugitive offender" means proceedings under section 9 of the Extradition Act 1870, section 7 of the Fugitive Offenders Act 1967 or section 2(1) or 4(3) of the Backing of Warrants (Republic of Ireland) Act 1965.

"Supreme Court rules" means rules made under section 99 of the Supreme Court of Judicature (Consolidation) Act 1925,

"surrender to custody" means, in relation to a person released on bail, surrendering himself into the custody of the court or of the constable (according to the requirements of the grant of bail) at the time and place for the time being appointed for him to do so,

"vary", in relation to bail, means imposing further conditions after bail is granted, or varying or rescinding conditions, "young person" means a person who has attained the age of fourteen and is under the age of seventeen.

(3) Where an enactment (whenever passed) which relates to bail in criminal proceedings refers to the person bailed appearing before a court it is to be construed unless the context otherwise requires as referring to his surrendering himself into the custody of the court.

(4) Any reference in this Act to any other enactment is a reference thereto as amended, and includes a reference thereto as extended or applied, by or under any other enactment, including this Act.

INCIDENTS OF BAIL IN CRIMINAL PROCEEDINGS

3. General provisions

(1) A person granted bail in criminal proceedings shall be under a duty to surrender to custody, and that duty is enforceable in accordance with section 6 of this Act.

(2) No recognizance for his surrender to custody shall be taken from him.

(3) Except as provided by this section—

(*a*) no security for his surrender to custody shall be taken from him,

(*b*) he shall not be required to provide a surety or sureties for his surrender to custody, and

(*c*) no other requirement shall be imposed on him as a condition of bail.

(4) He may be required, before release on bail, to provide a surety or sureties to secure his surrender to custody.

(5) If it appears that he is unlikely to remain in Great Britain until the time appointed for him to surrender to custody, he may be required, before release on bail, to give security for his surrender to custody.

The security may be given by him or on his behalf.

(6) He may be required (but only by a court) to comply, before release on bail or later, with such requirements as appear to the court to be necessary to secure that—

(*a*) he surrenders to custody,

(*b*) he does not commit an offence while on bail,

(*c*) he does not interfere with witnesses or otherwise obstruct the course of justice whether in relation to himself or any other person,

(*d*) he makes himself available for the purpose of enabling inquiries or a report to be made to assist the court in dealing with him for the offence.

(7) If a parent or guardian of a child or young person consents to be surety for the

child or young person for the purposes of this subsection, the parent or guardian may be required to secure that the child or young person complies with any requirement imposed on him by virtue of subsection (6) above, but—

> (*a*) no requirement shall be imposed on the parent or the guardian of a young person by virtue of this subsection where it appears that the young person will attain the age of seventeen before the time to be appointed for him to surrender to custody; and

> (*b*) the parent or guardian shall not be required to secure compliance with any requirement to which his consent does not extend and shall not, in respect of those requirements to which his consent does extend, be bound in a sum greater than £50.

(8) Where a court has granted bail in criminal proceedings [that court or, where that court has committed a person on bail to the Crown Court for trial or to be sentenced or otherwise dealt with, that court or the Crown Court may] on application—

> (*a*) by or on behalf of the person to whom [bail] was granted, or
> (*b*) by the prosecutor or a constable,

vary the conditions of bail or impose conditions in respect of bail which it has [been] granted unconditionally.

(9) This section is subject to subsection (3) of section 26 of the Magistrates' Courts Act 1952 (conditions of bail on remand for medical examination).

BAIL FOR ACCUSED PERSONS AND OTHERS

4. General right to bail of accused persons and others

(1) A person to whom this section applies shall be granted bail except as provided in Schedule 1 to this Act.

(2) This section applies to a person who is accused of an offence when—

> (*a*) he appears or is brought before a magistrates' court or the Crown Court in the course of or in connection with proceedings for the offence, or
> (*b*) he applies to a court for bail in connection with the proceedings.

This subsection does not apply as respects proceedings on or after a person's conviction of the offence or proceedings against a fugitive offender for the offence.

(3) This section also applies to a person who, having been convicted of an offence, appears or is brought before a magistrates' court to be dealt with under section 6 or section 16 of the Powers of Criminal Courts Act 1973 (breach of requirement of probation or community service order).

(4) This section also applies to a person who has been convicted of an offence and whose case is adjourned by the court for the purpose of enabling inquiries or a report to be made to assist the court in dealing with him for the offence.

(5) Schedule 1 to this Act also has effect as respects conditions of bail for a person to whom this section applies.

(6) In Schedule 1 to this Act "the defendant" means a person to whom this section applies and any reference to a defendant whose case is adjourned for inquiries or a report is a reference to a person to whom this section applies by virtue of subsection (4) above.

(7) This section is subject to section 8 of the Magistrates' Courts Act 1952 (restriction of bail by magistrates' court in cases of treason).

SUPPLEMENTARY

5. Supplementary provisions about decisions on bail

(1) Subject to subsection (2) below, where—

    (*a*) a court or constable grants bail in criminal proceedings, or

    (*b*) a court withholds bail in criminal proceedings from a person to whom section 4 of this Act applies, or

    (*c*) a court, officer of a court or constable appoints a time or place or a court or officer of a court appoints a different time or place for a person granted bail in criminal proceedings to surrender to custody, or

    (*d*) a court varies any conditions of bail or imposes conditions in respect of bail in criminal proceedings,

that court, officer or constable shall make a record of the decision in the prescribed manner and containing the prescribed particulars and, if requested to do so by the person in relation to whom the decision was taken, shall cause him to be given a copy of the record of the decision as soon as practicable after the record is made.

(2) Where bail in criminal proceedings is granted by endorsing a warrant of arrest for bail the constable who releases on bail the person arrested shall make the record required by subsection (1) above instead of the judge or justice who issued the warrant.

(3) Where a magistrates' court or the Crown Court—

    (*a*) withholds bail in criminal proceedings, or

    (*b*) imposes conditions in granting bail in criminal proceedings, or

    (*c*) varies any conditions of bail or imposes conditions in respect of bail in criminal proceedings,

and does so in relation to a person to whom section 4 of this Act applies, then the court shall, with a view to enabling him to consider making an application in the matter to another court, give reasons for withholding bail or for imposing or varying the conditions.

(4) A court which is by virtue of subsection (3) above required to give reasons for its decision shall include a note of those reasons in the record of its decision and

shall (except in a case where, by virtue of subsection (5) below, this need not be done) give a copy of that note to the person in relation to whom the decision was taken.

(5) The Crown Court need not give a copy of the note of the reasons for its decision to the person in relation to whom the decision was taken where that person is represented by counsel or a solicitor unless his counsel or solicitor requests the court to do so.

(6) Where a magistrates' court withholds bail in criminal proceedings from a person who is not represented by counsel or a solicitor, the court shall—

> (*a*) if it is committing him for trial to the Crown Court, inform him that he may apply to the High Court or to the Crown Court to be granted bail;

> (*b*) in any other case, inform him that he may apply to the High Court for that purpose.

(7) Where a person has given security in pursuance of section 3(5) above and a court is satisfied that he failed to surrender to custody then, unless it appears that he had reasonable cause for his failure, the court may order the forfeiture of the security.

(8) If a court orders the forfeiture of a security under subsection (7) above, the court may declare that the forfeiture extends to such amount less than the full value of the security as it thinks fit to order.

[(8A) An order under subsection (7) above shall, unless previously revoked, take effect at the end of twenty-one days beginning with the day on which it is made.

(8B) A court which has ordered the forfeiture of a security under subsection (7) above may, if satisfied on an application made by or on behalf of the person who gave it that he did after all have reasonable cause for his failure to surrender to custody, by order remit the forfeiture or declare that it extends to such amount less than the full value of the security as it thinks fit to order.

(8C) An application under subsection (8B) above may be made before or after the order for forfeiture has taken effect, but shall not be entertained unless the court is satisfied that the prosecution was given reasonable notice of the applicant's intention to make it.]

(9) A security which has been ordered to be forfeited by a court under subsection (7) above shall, to the extent of the forfeiture—

> (*a*) if it consists of money, be accounted for and paid in the same manner as a fine imposed by that court would be;

> (*b*) if it does not consist of money, be enforced by such magistrates' court as may be specified in the order.

[(9A) Where an order is made under subsection (8B) above after the order for forfeiture of the security in question has taken effect, any money which would have fallen to be repaid or paid over to the person who gave the security if the order under subsection (8B) had been made before the order for forfeiture took effect shall be repaid or paid over to him.]

(10) In this section "prescribed" means, in relation to the decision of a court or an officer of a court, prescribed by Supreme Court rules, Courts-Martial Appeal rules, Crown Court rules or magistrates' courts rules, as the case requires or, in relation to a decision of a constable, prescribed by direction of the Secretary of State.

6. Offence of absconding by person released on bail

(1) If a person who has been released on bail in criminal proceedings fails without reasonable cause to surrender to custody he shall be guilty of an offence.

(2) If a person who—

(*a*) has been released on bail in criminal proceedings, and
(*b*) having reasonable cause therefor, has failed to surrender to custody,

fails to surrender to custody at the appointed place as soon after the appointed time as is reasonably practicable he shall be guilty of an offence.

(3) It shall be for the accused to prove that he had reasonable cause for his failure to surrender to custody.

(4) A failure to give to a person granted bail in criminal proceedings a copy of the record of the decision shall not constitute a reasonable cause for that person's failure to surrender to custody.

(5) An offence under subsection (1) or (2) above shall be punishable either on summary conviction or as if it were a criminal contempt of court.

(6) Where a magistrates' court convicts a person of an offence under subsection (1) or (2) above the court may, if it thinks—

(*a*) that the circumstances of the offence are such that greater punishment should be inflicted for that offence than the court has power to inflict, or

(*b*) in a case where it commits that person for trial to the Crown Court for another offence, that it would be appropriate for him to be dealt with for the offence under subsection (1) or (2) above by the court before which he is tried for the other offence,

commit him in custody or on bail to the Crown Court for sentence.

(7) A person who is convicted summarily of an offence under subsection (1) or (2) above and is not committed to the Crown Court for sentence shall be liable to imprisonment for a term not exceeding 3 months or to a fine not exceeding £400 or to both and a person who is so committed for sentence or is dealt with as for such a contempt shall be liable to imprisonment for a term not exceeding 12 months or to a fine or to both.

(8) In any proceedings for an offence under subsection (1) or (2) above a document purporting to be a copy of the part of the prescribed record which relates

to the time and place appointed for the person specified in the record to surrender to custody and to be duly certified to be a true copy of that part of the record shall be evidence of the time and place appointed for that person to surrender to custody.

(9) For the purposes of subsection (8) above—

(*a*) "the prescribed record" means the record of the decision of the court, officer or constable made in pursuance of section 5(1) of this Act;

(*b*) the copy of the prescribed record is duly certified if it is certified by the appropriate officer of the court or, as the case may be, by the constable who took the decision or a constable designated for the purpose by the officer in charge of the police station from which the person to whom the record relates was released;

(*c*) "the appropriate officer" of the court is—

(i) in the case of a magistrates' court, the justices' clerk or such other officer as may be authorised by him to act for the purpose;

(ii) in the case of the Crown Court, such officer as may be designated for the purpose in accordance with arrangements made by the Lord Chancellor;

(iii) in the case of the High Court, such officer as may be designated for the purpose in accordance with arrangements made by the Lord Chancellor;

(iv) in the case of the Court of Appeal, the registrar of criminal appeals or such other officer as may be authorised by him to act for the purpose;

(v) in the case of the Courts-Martial Appeal Court, the registrar or such other officer as may be authorised by him to act for the purpose.

7. Liability to arrest for absconding or breaking conditions of bail

(1) If a person who has been released on bail in criminal proceedings and is under a duty to surrender into the custody of a court fails to surrender to custody at the time appointed for him to do so the court may issue a warrant for his arrest.

(2) If a person who has been released on bail in criminal proceedings absents himself from the court at any time after he has surrendered into the custody of the court and before the court is ready to begin or to resume the hearing of the proceedings, the court may issue a warrant for his arrest; but no warrant shall be issued under this subsection where that person is absent in accordance with leave given to him by or on behalf of the court.

(3) A person who has been released on bail in criminal proceedings and is under a duty to surrender into the custody of a court may be arrested without warrant by a constable—

(*a*) if the constable has reasonable grounds for believing that that person is not likely to surrender to custody;

(*b*) if the constable has reasonable grounds for believing that that person is likely to break any of the conditions of his bail or has reasonable grounds for suspecting that that person has broken any of those conditions; or

(*c*) in a case where that person was released on bail with one or more surety or sureties, if a surety notifies a constable in writing that that person is unlikely to surrender to custody and that for that reason the surety wishes to be relieved of his obligations as a surety.

(4) A person arrested in pursuance of subsection (3) above—

(*a*) shall, except where he was arrested within 24 hours of the time appointed for him to surrender to custody, be brought as soon as practicable and in any event within 24 hours after his arrest before a justice of the peace for the petty sessions area in which he was arrested; and

(*b*) in the said excepted case shall be brought before the court at which he was to have surrendered to custody.

[In reckoning for the purposes of this subsection any period of 24 hours, no account shall be taken of Christmas Day, Good Friday or any Sunday.]

(5) A justice of the peace before whom a person is brought under subsection (4) above may, subject to subsection (6) below, if of the opinion that that person—

(*a*) is not likely to surrender to custody, or

(*b*) has broken or is likely to break any condition of his bail,

remand him in custody or commit him to custody, as the case may require, or alternatively, grant him bail subject to the same or to different conditions, but if not of that opinion shall grant him bail subject to the same conditions (if any) as were originally imposed.

(6) Where the person so brought before the justice is a child or young person and the justice does not grant him bail, subsection (5) above shall have effect subject to the provisions of section 23 of the Children and Young Persons Act 1969 (remands to the care of local authorities).

8. Bail with sureties

(1) This section applies where a person is granted bail in criminal proceedings on condition that he provides one or more surety or sureties for the purpose of securing that he surrenders to custody.

(2) In considering the suitability for that purpose of a proposed surety, regard may be had (amongst other things) to—

(*a*) the surety's financial resources;

(*b*) his character and any previous convictions of his; and

(*c*) his proximity (whether in point of kinship, place of residence or otherwise) to the person for whom he is to be surety.

(3) Where a court grants a person bail in criminal proceedings on such a condition but is unable to release him because no surety or no suitable surety is available, the court shall fix the amount in which the surety is to be bound and subsections (4) and (5) below, or in a case where the proposed surety resides in Scotland subsection (6) below, shall apply for the purpose of enabling the recognizance of the surety to be entered into subsequently.

(4) Where this subsection applies the recognizance of the surety may be entered into before such of the following persons or descriptions of persons as the court may by order specify or, if it makes no such order, before any of the following persons, that is to say—

(a) where the decision is taken by a magistrates' court, before a justice of the peace, a justices' clerk or a police officer who either is of the rank of inspector or above or is in charge of a police station or, if magistrates' courts rules so provide, by a person of such other description as is specified in the rules;

(b) where the decision is taken by the Crown Court, before any of the persons specified in paragraph (a) above or, if Crown Court rules so provide, by a person of such other description as is specified in the rules;

(c) where the decision is taken by the High Court or the Court of Appeal, before any of the persons specified in paragraph (a) above or, if Supreme Court rules so provide, by a person of such other description as is specified in the rules;

(d) where the decision is taken by the Courts-Martial Appeal Court, before any of the persons specified in paragraph (a) above or, if Courts-Martial Appeal rules so provide, by a person of such other description as is specified in the rules;

and Supreme Court rules, Crown Court rules, Courts-Martial Appeal rules or magistrates' courts rules may also prescribe the manner in which a recognizance which is to be entered into before such a person is to be entered into and the persons by whom and the manner in which the recognizance may be enforced.

(5) Where a surety seeks to enter into his recognizance before any person in accordance with subsection (4) above but that person declines to take his recognizance because he is not satisfied of the surety's suitability, the surety may apply to—

(a) the court which fixed the amount of the recognizance in which the surety was to be bound, or

(b) a magistrates' court for the petty sessions area in which he resides,

for that court to take his recognizance and that court shall, if satisfied of his suitability, take his recognizance.

(6) Where this subsection applies, the court, if satisfied of the suitability of the

proposed surety, may direct that arrangements be made for the recognizance of the surety to be entered into in Scotland before any constable, within the meaning of the Police (Scotland) Act 1967, having charge at any police office or station in like manner as the recognizance would be entered into in England or Wales.

(7) Where, in pursuance of subsection (4) or (6) above, a recognizance is entered into otherwise than before the court that fixed the amount of the recognizance, the same consequences shall follow as if it had been entered into before that court.

MISCELLANEOUS

9. Offence of agreeing to indemnify sureties in criminal proceedings

(1) If a person agrees with another to indemnify that other against any liability which that other may incur as a surety to secure the surrender to custody of a person accused or convicted of or under arrest for an offence, he and that other person shall be guilty of an offence.

(2) An offence under subsection (1) above is committed whether the agreement is made before or after the person to be indemnified becomes a surety and whether or not he becomes a surety and whether the agreement contemplates compensation in money or in money's worth.

(3) Where a magistrates' court convicts a person of an offence under subsection (1) above the court may, if it thinks—

(a) that the circumstances of the offence are such that greater punishment should be inflicted for that offence than the court has power to inflict, or

(b) in a case where it commits that person for trial to the Crown Court for another offence, that it would be appropriate for him to be dealt with for the offence under subsection (1) above by the court before which he is tried for the other offence,

commit him in custody or on bail to the Crown Court for sentence.

(4) A person guilty of an offence under subsection (1) above shall be liable—

(a) on summary conviction, to imprisonment for a term not exceeding 3 months or to a fine not exceeding £400 or to both; or

(b) on conviction on indictment or if sentenced by the Crown Court on committal for sentence under subsection (3) above, to imprisonment for a term not exceeding 12 months or to a fine or to both.

(5) No proceedings for an offence under subsection (1) above shall be instituted except by or with the consent of the Director of Public Prosecutions.

10. Extension and Exercise of Coroner's powers to grant bail

[This section has been deleted by Criminal Law Act 1977, Sch 13.]

11. Legal aid for bail decisions in certain cases and for persons kept in custody for inquiries or reports

(1) Part II of the Legal Aid Act 1974 shall have effect subject to the amendments made by this section.

(2) In section 28(1) (exercise of powers to grant legal aid), for the words "subsections (2) to (4)" there shall be substituted the words "subsections (1A) to (4)".

(3) At the end of section 28(2) (power of magistrates' court to make a legal aid order in criminal proceedings), there shall be added the words "or, in the circumstances mentioned in paragraph (c) of section 29(1) below, for the purpose of so much of those proceedings as relates to the grant of bail".

(4) After paragraphs (a) and (b) of section 29(1) (which specify the cases in which a legal aid order must be made if a person's means qualify him for it), there shall be added a paragraph (preceded by the word "or") as follows—

"(c) where a person charged with an offence before a magistrates' court is brought before the court in pursuance of a remand in custody on an occasion when he may be again remanded or committed in custody and is not (but wishes to be) legally represented before the court, not having been legally represented before the court when he was so remanded".

(5) After paragraph (c) of section 29(1) inserted by subsection (4) above, there shall be added a further paragraph (preceded by the word "or") as follows—

"(d) where a person who is to be sentenced or dealt with for an offence by a magistrates' court or the Crown Court is to be kept in custody to enable inquiries or a report to be made to assist the court in sentencing or dealing with him for the offence;"

(6) After section 29(1) there shall be inserted the following subsection—

"(1A) Nothing in subsection (1) above shall require a magistrates' court, in the circumstances mentioned in paragraph (c) of that subsection, to order that the person charged before it be given legal aid for the purposes of the proceedings before that court and any juvenile court (as distinct from legal aid for the purpose of so much of those proceedings as relates to the grant of bail) or, in those circumstances, to make a legal aid order after the conviction of that person.";

(7) After section 29(5) there shall be inserted the following subsection—

"(5A) Paragraphs (c) and (d) of subsection (1) above shall have effect in their application to a person who has not attained the age of eighteen as if the references to a remand in custody and to being remanded, committed or kept in custody included references to being committed under section 23 of the Children and Young Persons Act 1969 to the care of a local authority or to a remand centre.";

(8) In section 30(2) (scope of legal aid before magistrates' courts) there shall be added at the end of the words "and legal aid ordered to be given for the purpose of so much of any proceedings before a magistrates' court as relates to the grant of bail shall not include representation by counsel."

(9) In section 30(12) (interpretation), for the words "In section 28 above" there shall be inserted the words "In sections 28 and 29 above".

12. Amendments, repeals and transitional provisions

(1) Schedule 2 to this Act (which contains consequential and minor amendments of enactments) shall have effect.

(2) The enactments specified in Schedule 3 to this Act are hereby repealed to the extent specified in the third column of that Schedule.

(3) The transitional provisions contained in Schedule 4 to this Act shall have effect.

13. Short title, commencement, application and extent

(1) This Act may be cited as the Bail Act 1976.

(2) This Act (except this section) shall come into force on such day as the Secretary of State may by order in a statutory instrument appoint.

(3) Section 1 of this Act applies to bail grantable by the Courts-Martial Appeal Court when sitting outside England and Wales and accordingly section 6 of this Act applies to a failure outside England and Wales by a person granted bail by that Court to surrender to custody.

(4) Except as provided by subsection (3) above and with the exception of so much of section 8 as relates to entering into recognizances in Scotland and paragraphs 31 and 46 of Schedule 2 to this Act, this Act does not extend beyond England and Wales.

SCHEDULES

SCHEDULE 1

PERSONS ENTITLED TO BAIL: SUPPLEMENTARY PROVISIONS

PART I

DEFENDANTS ACUSED OR CONVICTED OF IMPRISONABLE OFFENCES

Defendants to whom Part I applies

1. Where the offence or one of the offences of which the defendant is accused or convicted in the proceedings is punishable with imprisonment the following provisions of this Part of this Schedule apply.

Exceptions to right to bail

2. The defendant need not be granted bail if the court is satisfied that there are substantial grounds for believing that the defendant, if released on bail (whether subject to conditions or not) would—

    (*a*) fail to surrender to custody, or

    (*b*) commit an offence while on bail, or

    (*c*) interfere with witnesses or otherwise obstruct the course of justice, whether in relation to himself or any other person.

3. The defendant need not be granted bail if the court is satisfied that the defendant should be kept in custody for his own protection or, if he is a child or young person, for his own welfare.

4. The defendant need not be granted bail if he is in custody in pursuance of the sentence of a court or of any authority acting under any of the Services Acts.

5. The defendant need not be granted bail where the court is satisfied that it has not been practicable to obtain sufficient information for the purpose of taking the decisions required by this Part of this Schedule for want of time since the institution of the proceedings against him.

6. The defendant need not be granted bail if, having been released on bail in or in connection with the proceedings for the offence, he has been arrested in pursuance of section 7 of this Act.

Exception applicable only to defendant whose case is adjourned for inquiries or a report

7. Where his case is adjourned for inquiries or a report, the defendant need not be granted bail if it appears to the court that it would be impracticable to complete the inquiries or make the report without keeping the defendant in custody.

Restriction of conditions of bail

8.—(1) Subject to sub-paragraph (3) below, where the defendant is granted bail, no conditions shall be imposed under subsections (4) to (7) of section 3 of this Act unless it appears to the court that it is necessary to do so for the purpose of preventing the occurrence of any of the events mentioned in paragraph 2 of this Part of this Schedule or, in the case of a condition under subsection (6)(*d*) of that section, that it is necessary to impose it to enable inquiries or a report to be made into the defendant's physical or mental condition.

(2) Sub-paragraph (1) above also applies on any application to the court to vary the conditions of bail or to impose conditions in respect of bail which has been granted unconditionally.

(3) The restriction imposed by sub-paragraph (1) above shall not operate to override the direction in section 26(3) of the Magistrates' Courts Act 1952 to a magistrates' court to impose conditions of bail under section 3(6)(*d*) of this Act of the description specified in the said section 26(3) in the circumstances so specified.

Decisions under paragraph 2

9. In taking the decisions required by paragraph 2 of this Part of this Schedule, the court shall have regard to such of the following considerations as appear to it to be relevant, that is to say—

(*a*) the nature and seriousness of the offence or default (and the probable method of dealing with the defendant for it),

(*b*) the character, antecedents, associations and community ties of the defendant,

(*c*) the defendant's record as respects the fulfilment of his obligations under previous grants of bail in criminal proceedings,

(*d*) except in the case of a defendant whose case is adjourned for inquiries or a report, the strength of the evidence of his having committed the offence or having defaulted,

as well as to any others which appear to be relevant.

PART II

DEFENDANTS ACCUSED OR CONVICTED OF NON-IMPRISONABLE OFFENCES

Defendants to whom Part II applies

1. Where the offence or every offence of which the defendant is accused or convicted in the proceedings is one which is not punishable with imprisonment the following provisions of this Part of this Schedule apply.

Exceptions to right to bail

2. The defendant need not be granted bail if—

   (*a*) it appears to the court that, having been previously granted bail in criminal proceedings, he has failed to surrender to custody in accordance with his obligations under the grant of bail; and

   (*b*) the court believes, in view of that failure, that the defendant, if released on bail (whether subject to conditions or not) would fail to surrender to custody.

3. The defendant need not be granted bail if the court is satisfied that the defendant should be kept in custody for his own protection or, if he is a child or young person, for his own welfare.

4. The defendant need not be granted bail if he is in custody in pursuance of the sentence of a court or of any authority acting under any of the Services Acts.

5. The defendant need not be granted bail if, having been released on bail in or in connection with the proceedings for the offence, he has been arrested in pursuance of section 7 of this Act.

PART III

INTERPRETATION

1. For the purposes of this Schedule the question whether an offence is one which is punishable with imprisonment shall be determined without regard to any enactment prohibiting or restricting the imprisonment of young offenders or first offenders.

2. References in this Schedule to previous grants of bail in criminal proceedings include references to bail granted before the coming into force of this Act.

3. References in this Schedule to a defendant's being kept in custody or being in custody include (where the defendant is a child or young person) references to his being kept or being in the care of a local authority in pursuance of a warrant of commitment under section 23(1) of the Children and Young Persons Act 1969.

4. In this Schedule—

"court", in the expression "sentence of a court", includes a service court as defined in section 12(1) of the Visiting Forces Act 1952 and "sentence", in that expression, shall be construed in accordance with that definition;

"default", in relation to the defendant, means the default for which he is to be dealt with under section 6 or section 16 of the Powers of Criminal Courts Act 1973;

"the Services Acts" means the Army Act 1955, the Air Force Act 1955 and the Naval Discipline Act 1957.

SCHEDULE 2

CONSEQUENTIAL AND OTHER AMENDMENTS OF ACTS

Habeas Corpus Act 1679

1. In section 2 of the Habeas Corpus Act 1679 (bail for persons released from custody under habeas corpus while awaiting trial) for the words from "discharge the said prisoner" to "his or their appearance in" there shall be substituted the words "grant bail in accordance with the Bail Act 1976 to the said prisoner subject to a duty to appear before" and for the words "and the said recognizance or recognizances" there shall be substituted the words "together with the recognizance of any surety for him".

Metropolitan Police Act 1839

2. In section 69 (persons arrested to be kept in custody or bailed) for the words "give bail for his appearance" there shall be substituted the words "be granted bail subject to a duty to appear".

Criminal Law Amendment Act 1867

3. In section 10 of the Criminal Law Amendment Act 1867 (production from prison without habeas corpus where recognizances for appearance have been

taken) for the words from the beginning to "such court" there shall be substituted the words "Where a person who has been granted bail in criminal proceedings is, while awaiting trial for the offence before the Crown Court, in prison".

Interpretation Act 1889

5. In section 27 of the Interpretation Act 1889 (meaning of "committed for trial") for the words "to custody" wherever occurring there shall be substituted the words "in custody or on bail" and the words from "and shall include" to the end shall be omitted.

Perjury Act 1911

6. In section 9(1) of the Perjury Act 1911 (bail for person directed by the court to be prosecuted for perjury) for the words "admit him to bail" there shall be substituted the words "grant him bail".

Criminal Justice Administration Act 1914

7. In section 19 of the Criminal Justice Administration Act 1914 (continuous bail otherwise than in proceedings in magistrates' courts), for the words "the recognizance may be conditioned" there shall be substituted the words "the court may, where it remands him on bail in criminal proceedings (within the meaning of the Bail Act 1976) direct him to appear or, in any other case, direct that his recognizance be conditioned".

Indictments Act 1915

8. In section 5(5)(*c*) of the Indictments Act 1915 (bail where separate trial or postponed trial ordered) for the words "admitting the accused person to bail" there shall be substituted the words "granting the accused person bail".

Children and Young Persons Act 1933

9. In section 13(2) of the Children and Young Persons Act 1933 (police bail for person arrested for serious offence against juvenile) for the words from "on his entering" to the end there shall be substituted the words "on bail in accordance with the Bail Act 1976 subject to a duty to appear at the hearing of the charge".

Public Order Act 1936

10. In section 1(2) of the Public Order Act 1936 (right to release on bail in certain circumstances of persons charged with wearing uniforms in public), for the words "discharged from custody on entering into a recognizance" there shall be substituted the words "released on bail".

Criminal Justice Act 1948

11.—(1) Section 37 of the Criminal Justice Act 1948 (powers of High Court to grant bail on appeals against and other proceedings questioning convictions or sentences) shall be amended as follows.

(2) In subsection (1), in paragraph (*b*), for the words "release on bail" there shall be substituted the words "grant bail to".

(3) In subsection (1), for paragraph (*d*), there shall be substituted the following—

"(*d*) the High Court may grant bail to a person who has been convicted or sentenced by a magistrates' court and has applied to the High Court for an order of certiorari to remove the proceedings into the High Court or has applied to the High Court for leave to make such an application;".

(4) After subsection (1) there shall be inserted the following subsection—

"(1A) Where the court grants bail to a person under paragraph (*d*) of subsection (1) above—

(*a*) the time at which he is to appear in the event of the conviction or sentence not being quashed by the High Court shall be such time within ten days after the judgment of the High Court has been given as may be specified by the High Court; and

(*b*) the place at which he is to appear in that event shall be a magistrates' court acting for the same petty sessions area as the court which convicted or sentenced him."

(5) In subsection (6), for the words "admitted to" wherever occurring there shall be substituted the words "released on".

Representation of the People Act 1949

12. In section 149(7) of the Representation of the People Act 1949 (bail by election court ordering trial before magistrates' court of offences disclosed on an election petition) for the words "cause him to give bail" there shall be substituted the words "grant him bail in accordance with the Bail Act 1976 subject to a duty".

Diseases of Animals Act 1950

13. In section 71(4) of the Diseases of Animals Act 1950 (application of enactments about release on bail by police) for the words "recognizances taken" there shall be substituted the word "bail".

Magistrates' Courts Act 1952

14. In section 7 of the Magistrates' Courts Act 1952 (discharge or committal for trial) (in this Schedule referred to as "the Act of 1952") for subsection (2) there shall be substituted the following subsection—

"(2) Subject to section 4 of the Bail Act 1976 and section 8 of this Act, the court may commit a person for trial—

   (*a*) in custody, that is to say, by committing him to custody there to be safely kept until delivered in due course of law, or

   (*b*) on bail in accordance with the Bail Act 1976, that is to say, by directing him to appear before the Crown Court for trial;

and where his release on bail is conditional on his providing one or more surety or sureties and, in accordance with section 8(3) of the Bail Act 1976, the court fixes the amount in which the surety is to be bound with a view to his entering into his recognizance subsequently in accordance with subsections (4) and (5) or (6) of that section the court shall in the meantime commit the accused to custody in accordance with paragraph (*a*) of this subsection.".

15. In section 7(3) of the Act of 1952 (bail after committal for trial), for the words from "release" to the end, there shall be substituted the words "grant him bail in accordance with the Bail Act 1976 subject to a duty to appear before the Crown Court for trial."

16. In section 8 of the Act of 1952 (bail in treason) for the words "admitted to" there shall be substituted the word "granted".

17. In section 26 of the Act of 1952 (remand for medical examination), for subsection (3) there shall be substituted the following—

"(3) Where on an adjournment under subsection (1) above the accused is remanded on bail, the court shall impose conditions under paragraph (*d*) of section 3(6) of the Bail Act 1976 and the requirements imposed as conditions under that paragraph shall be or shall include requirements that the accused—

   (*a*) undergo medical examination by a duly qualified medical practitioner or, where the inquiry is into his mental condition and the court so directs, two such practitioners; and

   (*b*) for that purpose attend such an institution or place, or on such practitioner as the court directs and, where the inquiry is into his mental condition, comply with any other directions which may be given to him for that purpose by any person specified by the court or by a person of any class so specified".

18. In section 38(1) of the Act of 1952 (bail on arrest without warrant), for the words from "release" to the end there shall be substituted the words "grant him bail in accordance with the Bail Act 1976 subject to a duty to appear before a magistrates' court at such time and place as the officer appoints".

19. After section 38(1) of the Act of 1952 there shall be inserted the following subsection—

"(1A) Where a person has been granted bail under subsection (1) above, the magistrates' court before which he is to appear may appoint a later time as the time at which he is to appear and may enlarge the recognizances of any sureties for him to that time."

20. In section 38(2) of the Act of 1952, for the words from "release" to "recognizance" in the second place where it occurs, there shall be substituted the words "grant him bail in accordance with the Bail Act 1976 subject to a duty to appear at such a police station and at such a time as the officer appoints" and for the words "any such recognizance" there shall be substituted the words "the recognizance of any surety for that person".

21. Section 38(3) of the Act of 1952 (recognizance by parent or guardian on release of child or young person on bail) shall be omitted.

22. In section 89(1) of the Act of 1952 (terms of bail on appeal or case stated)—

(a) for the words from "release" to "conditioned" there shall be substituted the words "grant him bail."; and

(b) for paragraphs (a) and (b) there shall be substituted the following subsection—

"(1A) If a person is granted bail under subsection (1) above, the time and place at which he is to appear (except in the event of the determination in respect of which the case is stated being reversed by the High Court) shall be—

(a) if he has given notice of appeal, the Crown Court at the time appointed for the hearing of the appeal;

(b) if he has applied for the statement of a case, the magistrates' court at such time within ten days after the judgment of the High Court has been given as may be specified by the magistrates' court;

and any recognizance that may be taken from him or from any surety for him shall be conditioned accordingly."

23. In section 89(3) of the Act of 1952 (computation of sentence where bail granted pending hearing of case stated), for the words "admitted to" wherever occurring there shall be substituted the words "released on".

24. For section 93 of the Act of 1952 (warrants endorsed for bail), there shall be substituted the following—

"93.—(1) A justice of the peace on issuing a warrant for the arrest of any person may grant him bail by endorsing the warrant for bail, that is to say, by endorsing the warrant with a direction in accordance with subsection (2) below.

(2) A direction for bail endorsed on a warrant under subsection (1) above shall—

(a) in the case of bail in criminal proceedings, state that the person arrested is to be released on bail subject to a duty to appear before such magistrates' court and at such time as may be specified in the endorsement;

(*b*) in the case of bail otherwise than in criminal proceedings, state that the person arrested is to be released on bail on his entering into such a recognizance (with or without sureties) conditioned for his appearance before a magistrates' court as may be specified in the endorsement;

and the endorsement shall fix the amounts in which any sureties and, in a case falling within paragraph (*b*) above, that person is or are to be bound.

(3) Where a warrant has been endorsed for bail under subsection (1) above, then, on the person referred to in the warrant being taken to a police station on arrest under the warrant, the officer in charge of the police station shall (subject to his approving any surety tendered in compliance with the endorsement) release him from custody as directed in the endorsement.".

25. At the end of section 94 of the Act of 1952 (variation of terms of bail), there shall be added the following words—

"Provided that this section does not apply in relation to a person granted bail in criminal proceedings".

26. In section 105 of the Act of 1952 (exercise of powers to remand in custody or on bail), for subsection (1) there shall be substituted the following—

"(1) Where a magistrates' court has power to remand any person, then, subject to section 4 of the Bail Act 1976 and to any other enactment modifying that power, the court may—

(*a*) remand him in custody, that is to say, commit him to custody to be brought before the court at the end of the period of remand or at such earlier time as the court may require; or

(*b*) where it is inquiring into or trying an offence alleged to have been committed by that person or has convicted him of an offence, remand him on bail in accordance with the Bail Act 1976, that is to say, by directing him to appear as provided in subsection (3) of this section; or

(*c*) except in a case falling within paragraph (*b*) above, remand him on bail by taking from him a recognizance (with or without sureties) conditioned as provided in that subsection;

and may, in a case falling within paragraph (*c*) above, instead of taking recognizances in accordance with that paragraph, fix the amount of the recognizances with a view to their being taken subsequently in accordance with section 95 of this Act.

(1A) Where the court fixes the amount of a recognizance under subsection (1) of this section or section 8(3) of the Bail Act 1976 with a view to its being taken subsequently the court shall in the meantime commit the person so remanded to custody in accordance with paragraph (*a*) of the said subsection (1).".

27. In section 105 of the Act of 1952, for subsection (3) there shall be substituted the following—

"(3) Where a person is remanded on bail under subsection (1) of this section the court may, where it remands him on bail in accordance with the Bail Act 1976 direct him to appear or, in any other case, direct that his recognizance be conditioned for his appearance—

(*a*) before that court at the end of the period of remand; or

(*b*) at every time and place to which during the course of the proceedings the hearing may be from time to time adjourned;

and, where it remands him on bail conditionally on his providing a surety during an inquiry into an offence alleged to have been committed by him, may direct that the recognizance of the surety be conditioned to secure that the person so bailed appears—

(*c*) at every time and place to which during the course of the proceedings the hearing may be from time to time adjourned and also before the Crown Court in the event of the person so bailed being committed for trial there.

(3A) Where a person is directed to appear or a recognizance is conditioned for a person's appearance in accordance with paragraph (*b*) or (*c*) of subsection (3) of this section, the fixing at any time of the time for him next to appear shall be deemed to be a remand; but nothing in this or the last preceding subsection shall deprive the court of power at any subsequent hearing to remand him afresh.".

28.—(1) Section 106 of the Act of 1952 (further remands) shall be amended as follows.

(2) In subsection (2), for the words after "further time" there shall be substituted the words—

"(*a*) where he was granted bail in criminal proceedings, includes power to enlarge the recognizance of any surety for him to a later time;

(*b*) where he was granted bail otherwise than in criminal proceedings, may be exercised by enlarging his recognizance and those of any sureties for him to a later time."

(3) For subsection (3), there shall be substituted the following subsection—

"(3) Where a person remanded on bail is bound to appear before a magistrates' court at any time and the court has no power to remand him under subsection (1) of this section, the court may in his absence—

(*a*) where he was granted bail in criminal proceedings, appoint a later time

as the time at which he is to appear and enlarge the recognizances of
any sureties for him to that time;

(b) where he was granted bail otherwise than in criminal proceedings,
enlarge his recognizance and those of any sureties for him to a later
time;

and the appointment of the time or the enlargement of his recognizance shall
be deemed to be a further remand."

(4) At the end of the section there shall be added the following subsection—

"(4) Where a magistrates' court commits a person for trial on bail and the
recognizance of any surety for him has been conditioned in accordance with
paragraph (a) of subsection (3) of the last preceding section the court may, in
the absence of the surety, enlarge his recognizance so that he is bound to secure
that the person so committed for trial appears also before the Crown Court.".

29. In section 126(1) of the Act of 1952 (definitions), there shall be inserted at the
appropriate place the following definition—

"'bail in criminal proceedings' has the same meaning as in the Bail Act 1976".

Administration of Justice Act 1960

30. In section 4(2) of the Administration of Justice Act 1960 (power to grant bail
in appeals from Divisional Courts), after the words "in relation to" there shall be
inserted the words "the time and place of appearance appointed and" and, after the
words "entered into", there shall be inserted the words "by any surety".

31. In section 6(1) of the Administration of Justice Act 1960 (computation of
sentence where bail granted in appeals to House of Lords) for the words "admitted
to" there shall be substituted the word "granted" and for the words "at large after
being so admitted" there shall be substituted the words "released on bail".

32. In section 16(2) of the Administration of Justice Act 1960 (variation of
sentence on certiorari) for the words "at large after being admitted to bail" there
shall be substituted the words "released on bail".

Backing of Warrants (Republic of Ireland) Act 1965

33.—(1) Section 5 of the Backing of Warrants (Republic of Ireland) Act 1965
shall be amended as follows.

(2) In subsection (1), for paragraph (b) and the words following that paragraph
there shall be substituted the following—

"(b) remand him on bail in accordance with the Bail Act 1976, that is to say,
direct him to surrender himself into the custody of the officer in charge of
a specified police station at the time to be appointed by that officer and
notified in writing to the person so remanded;

and where his release on bail is conditional on his providing one or more surety or sureties and, in accordance with section 8(3) of that Act, the court fixes the amount in which the surety is to be bound with a view to his entering into his recognizance subsequently in accordance with subsections (4) and (5) or (6) of that section the court shall in the meantime commit him to the custody of a constable."

(3) In subsection (2), there shall be substituted, for the words from the beginning to "so served" the words "The time to be appointed for the purposes of subsection (1) above by the officer and notified to the person so remanded".

(4) In subsection (3), for the words from "release" to the end there shall be substituted the words "grant him bail in accordance with the Bail Act 1976 subject to a duty to surrender himself into the custody of the officer in charge of the station specified under subsection (1) above at the time appointed by that officer and notified in writing to him; and subsection (2) above shall apply to the appointment of a time for the purposes of this subsection as it applies to the appointment of a time for the purposes of subsection (1) above."

(5) In subsection (4), for the words "in the recognizance" there shall be substituted the words "under subsection (1) above" and for the words "release him" there shall be substituted the words "grant him bail".

Criminal Justice Act 1967

34. Section 18 of the Criminal Justice Act 1967 (restrictions on refusal of bail by magistrates' courts in criminal proceedings) shall be omitted.

35. In section 19(1) of the Criminal Justice Act 1967 (restriction on justices sitting after dealing with bail) for the words "the question of the defendant's admission to bail" there shall be substituted the words "whether the defendant shall be granted bail".

36. Section 21 of the Criminal Justice Act 1967 (power to impose special conditions of bail) shall be omitted.

37.—(1) Section 22 of the Criminal Justice Act 1967 (extension of power of High Court to grant, or vary conditions of, bail) shall be amended as follows.

(2) For subsections (1) and (2) there shall be substituted the following—

"(1) Where an inferior court withholds bail in criminal proceedings or imposes conditions in granting bail in criminal proceedings, the High Court may grant bail or vary the conditions.

(2) Where the High Court grants a person bail under this section it may direct him to appear at a time and place which the inferior court could have directed and the recognizance of any surety shall be conditioned accordingly."

(3) In subsection (3) for the words "admitted to" wherever occurring there shall be substituted the word "granted".

(4) At the end of subsection (4) there shall be added the words "'bail in criminal proceedings' and 'vary' have the same meanings as they have in the Bail Act 1976."

Criminal Appeal Act 1968

38. In section 8(2) and (3) of the Criminal Appeal Act 1968 (bail etc on retrial), for the words "admission to" there shallbe substituted the words "release on".

39. In section 16(3) of the Criminal Appeal Act 1968 (orders pending trial on reversal of finding of unfitness) for the words "admission to" there shall be substituted the words "release on".

40. In section 19 of the Criminal Appeal Act 1968 (bail on appeal to Court of Appeal) for the words "admit him to" there shall be substituted the words "grant him".

41. In section 29(3) of the Criminal Appeal Act 1968 (computation of sentence where bail granted by Court of Appeal) for the words "admitted to" there shall be substituted the word "granted" and for the words "at large after being so admitted" there shall be substituted the words "released on bail".

42. In section 31(2) of the Criminal Appeal Act 1968 (powers of Court of Appeal exercisable by single judge), for paragraph (*e*), there shall be substituted the following—

   "(*e*) to grant bail to an appellant".

43. In section 36 of the Criminal Appeal Act 1968 (bail on appeal from Court of Appeal) for the words "admit him to" there shall be substituted the words "grant him".

44. In section 43(1) of the Criminal Appeal Act 1968 (computation of sentence where bail granted on appeal to House of Lords) for the words "admitted to" there shall be substituted the word "granted" and for the words "at large after being so admitted" there shall be substituted the words "released on bail".

45. In Schedule 2 to the Criminal Appeal Act 1968 (provisions about retrial) in paragraph 2(3)(*b*) for the words "at large after being admitted to bail" there shall be substituted the words "released on bail".

Courts-Martial (Appeals) Act 1968

46. In section 45(2) of the Courts-Martial (Appeals) Act 1968 (computation of sentence where bail granted on appeal to House of Lords) for the words "admitted to" there shall be substituted the word "granted" and for the words "at large after being so admitted" there shall be substituted the words "released on bail".

Children and Young Persons Act 1969

47. In section 29 of the Children and Young Persons Act 1969, (release or further

detention of arrested child or young person), for subsection (2), there shall be substituted the following—

"(2) Where a parent or guardian enters into a recognizance to secure that the child or young person appears at the hearing of the charge, the recognizance may, if the said officer thinks fit, be conditioned for the attendance of the parent or guardian at the hearing in addition to the person arrested.";

and subsection (6) shall be omitted.

Courts Act 1971

48.—(1) Section 13 of the Courts Act 1971 (bail in the Crown Court) shall be amended as follows.

(2) At the beginning of subsection (1) there shall be inserted the words "Any direction to appear and" and after the words "specified in the", there shall be inserted the word "direction.".

(3) In subsection (4), for the words preceding the paragraphs there shall be substituted the words "The Crown Court may grant bail to any person—", and for the words "admitted to" there shall be substituted the words "released on".

(4) For subsection (5)(*a*) there shall be substituted the following paragraph—

"(*a*) except in the case of bail in criminal proceedings, allowing the court, instead of requiring a person to enter into a recognizance, to consent to his giving other security."

(5) At the end of subsection (6) there shall be added the following words—

"Provided that in the case of bail in criminal proceedings, the person arrested shall not be required to enter into a recognizance."

(6) At the end of the section there shall be added the following subsection—

"(10) In this section 'bail in criminal proceedings' has the same meaning as in the Bail Act 1976'".

SCHEDULE 3

REPEALS

Chapter	Short Title	Extent of Repeal
31 Chas. 2. c. 2.	The Habeas Corpus Act 1679.	In section 5, the words "by recognizance".
32 Geo. 3. c. 56.	The Servants' Characters Act 1792.	In section 6, the words "and enter into recognizance".
2 & 3 Vict. c. 47.	The Metropolitan Police Act 1839.	In section 69, the words from "to take bail" to the end.
2 & 3 Vict. c. 71.	The Metropolitan Police Courts Act 1839.	Section 36.
52 & 53 Vict. c. 63.	The Interpretation Act 1889.	In section 27, the words from "and shall include" to the end.
11 & 12 Geo. 6. c. 58.	The Criminal Justice Act 1948.	In section 37, subsections (2) and (3) and, in subsection (4), paragraph (*a*).
15 & 16 Geo. 6. & 1 Eliz. 2. c. 55.	The Magistrates' Courts Act 1952.	In section 16(2), the words "to enter into a recognizance or". In section 26, subsection (4). Section 38(3). Section 97.
8 & 9 Eliz. 2. c. 65.	The Administration of Justice Act 1960.	In section 4(3), the words "the applicant or".
1965 c. 45.	The Backing of Warrants (Republic of Ireland) Act 1965.	In section 5(4) the words "in breach of a recognizance taken from him under this section" and "without prejudice to the enforcement of the recognizance".
1967 c. 80.	The Criminal Justice Act 1967.	Sections 18 and 21. In section 22(3), the reference to subsection (3) of section 37 of the Criminal Justice Act 1948. Section 23.
1969 c. 54.	The Children and Young Persons Act 1969.	In section 29, subsection (6).
1971 c. 23.	The Courts Act 1971.	In section 13, subsection (3).
1972 c. 71.	The Criminal Justice Act 1972.	Section 43.

SCHEDULE 4

Transitional Provisions

1.—(1) Without prejudice to section 38(2) of the Interpretation Act 1889 (effect of repeals), nothing in the amendments or repeals effected by section 12 of and Schedules 2 and 3 to this Act shall affect the application of the enactments amended or repealed thereby in relation to recognizances entered into or security given by persons granted bail before the appointed day and the recognizances of any sureties for them.

(2) Nothing in those amendments or repeals shall, in particular, affect the doing of any of the following things after the appointed day, that is to say—

   (*a*) the enforcement of the recognizance of such a person in the event of a breach of recognizance after the appointed day;

   (*b*) the exercise of any power to issue and the execution of a warrant for the arrest of such a person for breach of his recognizance after the appointed day;

   (*c*) the exercise of any power to enlarge the recognizance of such a person and of any surety for him to a later time in the absence of that person and his surety (if any);

   (*d*) the exercise of any power to vary any conditions on which a person was granted bail before the appointed day or to reduce the amount in which he or any surety is to be bound or to discharge or dispense with any of the sureties;

and no application shall be made under section 3(8) of this Act for the variation of conditions of bail so granted or for the imposition of conditions in respect of bail so granted.

2. Where, before the appointed day, a court has—

   (*a*) given a direction that the recognizance of a person to whom it has granted bail may be entered into before another court or any person, or

   (*b*) endorsed a warrant for the arrest of a person with a direction that he be released on his entering into such a recognizance as is specified in the endorsement,

the recognizance may be entered into and taken after the appointed day in accordance with the direction and paragraph 1 above shall apply to such a recognizance as it applies to a recognizance entered into before the appointed day.

3. Where a person has been granted bail before the appointed day and his recognizance (and that of any surety for him) is conditioned for his appearance before a court from time to time, then, on his first appearance before a court after the appointed day—

(*a*) the recognizance of that person shall be discharged; and

(*b*) the recognizance of any surety for him shall, as directed by the court, either be discharged or continue in force.

4. In this Schedule "the appointed day" means the day appointed under section 13(2) of this Act for it to come into force.

Appendix B
Forms

Appendix B

1. NOTICE OF BAIL DECISION BY MAGISTRATES' COURTS

RECORD OF BAIL DECISION

(Bail Act, 1976 s5; M.C. Rules, 1968 rr 54, 75A Magistrates' Courts Act, 1952, s.38)

.... MAGISTRATES' COURT ( )

Date: _____

Accused: _____   Date of birth: _____

Last bail/custody
decision (if any)
(date):

Alleged offence(s):
(Short particulars
and statute)

Stage reached
in proceedings:

Decision:

1 The accused is granted bail with a duty to surrender to the custody of

2 The Court having found that the exception(s) to the right to bail specified in the first column of Schedule I hereto applies (apply) for the reason(s) specified in the second column of the said Schedule I, witholds bail.

   The accused is (remanded in) (committed to) custody for appearance before

3 The accused having been granted bail by the above Magistrates' Court

   on .... with a duty to surrender to the custody of:

4 (................Magistrates' Court on .... at .... am/pm)
   (the Crown Court on such a day and at such time and place as may be notified to the accused by the appropriate office of that Court)

5 the bail being subject to the conditions set out in Schedules II and III hereto

Application having been made by .... under section 3(8) of the Bail Act 1976 for (variation) (imposition) of bail conditions.

The conditions to be complied with by the accused in respect of the said bail shall now be as specified in Schedules II and III hereto

7   The conditions of bail were (varied) (imposed) for the following reasons:

....
(Justice of the Peace) (Clerk of the
Court present during these proceedings)

SCHEDULE I

Exception(s) as to right to bail (✓ *as appropriate*)	Reason(s) for applying the exception(s) specified in first column (*delete as appropriate*)
Pt I Para 2(a)	Nature and seriousness of offence and likely sentence or order.
Pt I Para 2(b)	
Pt I Para 2(c)	
Pt I Para 3	Character, antecedents, associates and community ties of accused
Pt I Para 4	
Pt I Para 5	
Pt I Para 6	Previous breaches of bail in criminal proceedings
Pt I Para 7	
Pt II Para 2(a)	Strength of evidence of having committed offence or defaulted
Pt II Para 2(b)	
Pt II Para 3	
Pt II Para 4	
Pt II Para 5	

SCHEDULE II

Conditions to be complied with before release on bail:

To provide .... suret(y)(ies) in the

sum of £ .... (each) to secure the accused's surrender to custody at the time and place appointed.

SCHEDULE III

Conditions to be complied with after release on bail:

2. NOTICE OF BAIL APPLICATION TO CROWN COURT

IN THE CROWN COURT

APPLICATION FOR BAIL

Take notice that an application relating to bail will be made to the Crown Court
at   on   at   am/pm
on behalf of the defendant/appellant/prosecutor/respondent

Name of Defendant/Appellant:
(block letters)

Crown Court reference number:

Solicitor for the Applicant:

Address:

If Defendant/Appellant is in custody
state place of detention and give
Prison No. if applicable:

State particulars of proceedings
during which Defendant/Appellant
was committed to custody or bailed
(un)conditionally:

Enter details of any relevant previous
applications for bail or variation of
conditions of bail:

Nature and grounds of application:
(State fully facts relied on and list
previous convictions (if any). Give details of any proposed sureties and
answer any objections raised previously):

3. SUMMONS FOR BAIL APPLICATION BEFORE JUDGE IN CHAMBERS [Form 97]

IN THE HIGH COURT OF JUSTICE

QUEEN'S BENCH DIVISION

Let all the parties concerned attend the Judge in Chambers on the   day

of   19   at   o'clock on the hearing of an

application on behalf of

to be granted bail as to his commitment

on the   day of   19   by a Magistrates'

Court sitting at

Dated the   day of   19

This summons was taken out by

of

Solicitors for the said

Appendix B

4. SUMMONS FOR APPLICATION FOR VARIATION IN BAIL CONDITIONS BEFORE JUDGE IN CHAMBERS [Form 97A]

IN THE HIGH COURT OF JUSTICE

QUEEN'S BENCH DIVISION

Let all parties concerned attend the Judge in Chambers on the   day of

      19   at   o'clock on the hearing of an

application (on behalf of   ) (by

) that the terms on which

      was granted bail by   on

should be varied as follows:

Terms on which   was granted bail:

Proposed variation:

Dated the   day of   of 19

This summons was taken out by (of)

(agent for   of)

solicitor for the said

((as prosecutor) (a constable of   Police Force)).

5. ORDER OF JUDGE IN CHAMBERS FOR RELEASE ON BAIL
[Form 98]

IN THE HIGH COURT OF JUSTICE

QUEEN'S BENCH DIVISION

The Honourable Mr. Justice   Judge in
Chambers. Whereas on the   day of   19

by a Magistrates' Court sitting at   for trial at the Crown
Court at   on a charge of

or was convicted by a Magistrates' Court sitting at
of   and sentenced to
and the said   has given notice of
appeal to the Crown Court against such conviction or sentence:

And whereas the said   is in the custody of the
Governor of Her Majesty's Prison at   and has
applied to the Judge in Chambers to be granted bail:

Upon hearing Counsel (or the Solicitor) for the said
          and upon reading the affidavit of
        filed the   day of   19

It is ordered that the said   after
complying with the condition(s) specified in Schedule 1 hereto, shall be released on
bail, subject to the condition(s) specified in Schedule II hereto, and with a duty to
surrender to the custody of the Magistrates' Court at
        on the   day of   19   at
        am/pm (the Crown Court on such day and at such time and place as
may be notified to the said   by the
appropriate officer of that Court)

Dated the   day of   19

[For the Schedules to this form see p64]

SCHEDULE I

Conditions to be complied with before release on bail

To provide   suret(y)(ies) in the sum of £   (each)

before a Justice of the peace (or as may be) to secure

surrender to custody at the time and place appointed.

SCHEDULE II

Conditions to be complied with after release on bail

6. ORDER BY A JUDGE IN CHAMBERS TO VARY CONDITIONS OF BAIL [Form 98A]

IN THE HIGH COURT OF JUSTICE

QUEEN'S BENCH DIVISION

The Honourable Mr. Justice   Judge in

Chambers whereas on the   day of   19

                                                by a Magistrates' Court

sitting at   for trial at the Crown Court at

                        on a charge of

or was convicted by a Magistrates' Court sitting at

of   and sentenced to

and the said   has given notice of appeal to the

Crown Court against such conviction or sentence:

And whereas the said   was granted bail with a

duty to surrender to the custody of (the Magistrates' Court at

                    on   at   am/pm) (the

Crown Court on a day and a time and place to be notified by the appropriate officer

of that Court) and subject to the following conditions:

And whereas (the said   )

((as prosecutor) (a constable of

Police Force) has applied to the Judge in Chambers for a variation in the said

arrangements for bail:

Upon hearing Counsel (or the solicitor) for the applicant and upon reading the

affidavit of   filed the

day of   19

It is ordered that the said arrangements for bail be varied as follows:

dated the   day of   19

Appendix B

7. NOTICE OF APPLICATION FOR BAIL TO COURT OF APPEAL, CRIMINAL DIVISION [Form B]

| SEE NOTES ON BACK | **B** | **CRIMINAL APPEAL ACT, 1968** | (See R 3 Form 4) |

COURT OF APPEAL CRIMINAL DIVISION

NOTICE OF APPLICATION FOR BAIL

To the Registrar, Criminal Appeal Office

REF. No.

Royal Courts of Justice, Strand, LONDON WC2A 2LL

Write legibly in black

Particulars of APPELLANT

FULL NAMES
Block letters

FORENAMES

SURNAME

ADDRESS
If detained give address where detained

INDEX NUMBER if detained

APPELLANT
(See Note 6)

Address if granted Bail

Amount of Recognizance offered

£ —————

SURETIES
(See Note 7)

Name, addresses, occupations

Amount of Recognizance offered

£ —————

£ —————

If bail was granted before trial or sentence state:

Amounts of Recognizances	APPELLANT	SURETIES	
	£	£	and £

Were the sureties the persons named above?

What, if any, special conditions were imposed?

The appellant applies for bail pending appeal/retrial on the following grounds:-

_____

_____

_____

_____

_____

_____

(Signed)	DATE	Address of person signing on behalf of appellant (See Note 5)
(Appellant)		

B	FOR USE IN THE CRIMINAL APPEAL OFFICE
	Received

Form 1455 31428—4-5-70 XBD

B CRIMINAL APPEAL ACT, 1968 R.3 Form 4

NOTES

1. This form must accompany or follow Form N. If this form follows Form N the Criminal Appeal reference number must be given. An application for bail may be made whether or not Form N contained an application for bail.

2. An application for bail will be considered in the light of the grounds of appeal or application for leave to appeal. Accordingly, it is usual for the application for bail to be submitted to the court or judge together with the other applications and the transcript of the proceedings at the trial. This imposes some delay. Generally, strong grounds of appeal or application for leave to appeal have to be shown before bail is granted.

3. Do not repeat the grounds of appeal or application for leave to appeal as the grounds for bail. Mention any special other grounds which the judge or court might consider, e.g., medical reasons.

4. Time spent on bail does not count towards sentence.

5. This form must be signed by or on behalf of the appellant. Any person signing on behalf of the appellant must give his address and status.

6. Give the appellant's address if bail were granted, and the amount of the recognizance in which he would agree to be bound.

7. Give the names, addresses and occupations of two persons who might act as sureties if bail were granted and the amounts of the recognizance in which they might agree to be bound.

Index